Immensity

Immensity

Poems by

Beth Paulson

Kelsay Books

© 2016 Beth Paulson. All rights reserved. This material may not be reproduced in any form, published, reprinted, recorded, performed, broadcast, rewritten or redistributed without the explicit permission of Beth Paulson. All such actions are strictly prohibited by law.

Photo taken by the Hubble Space Telescope, February 16, 2013.

http://www.reuters.com/news/picture/images-from-hubble?articleId=USRTR2D9GV
(accessed July5, 2016)

Cover Art: Star cluster NGC 2060, a loose collection of stars in 30 Doradus, located in the heart of the Tarantula Nebula 170,000 light-years away from Earth in the Large Magellanic Cloud, a small, satellite galaxy of the Milky Way.

ISBN 978-1-945752-03-2

Kelsay Books
Aldrich Press
www.kelsaybooks.com

Acknowledgments

Cloudbank: "Van Gogh at the Café in Arles"
Common Ground Review: "Each Life Converges to Some Centre" (Second Place)
Crosswinds: "February Day"
Dash: "I Reread an Old Poem"
Earth's Daughters: "Late Spring Under Whitehouse Mountain"
Emrys Journal: "The Heart of Matter"
Front Range Review: "Reflections on the Universal Law of Gravitation," "Tree Line"
Glassworks Magazine: "No Imminent Danger"
Grand Valley Magazine: "Ice Lakes"
Innisfree: "Last Time," "Erasure"
The Kerf: "Gentians"
Lindenwood Review: "Das a Luz"
Naugatuck River Review: "The Bear Woman," "Still Life With Oranges," (Third Place)
Off the Coast: "Ablation"
Passager: "Chance"
The Progenitor: "Exoplanet"
Red Rock Review: "At the Great Gallery"
Sierra Nevada Review: "All or Nothing"
Still Crazy: "Security Line"
Trajectory: "Summer 1968," "To Let the World Go"
Westview: "Animal Ways"
Willowcreek Review: "Monsoon Season"

I wish to express my deep gratitude to K.C. Cole whose insightful and clear writing about physics, quantum to cosmic, have informed and excited me for years. Also, thank you to poet Kim Addonizio who admonished me to keep digging deeper.

Thank you, Kierstin Bridger and Judith Terzi, often first readers of many of these poems, who always knew what I was about. And a special thank you to the Poetica poets of Ridgway, Colorado for their dedication and encouragement.

Finally, I thank Don, the love of my life, for his help with the hard science and so much more.

Contents

Immensity

Driving the Pass	15
Reflection on the Universal Law of Gravitation	16
Exoplanet	17
Ice Lakes	18
Immensity	19
Tree Line	20
Wolves	22
All or Nothing	24
Each Life Converges to Some Centre	26
At the Great Gallery	28
Solo Hiking, Utah	29
The Heart of Matter	30
Ten Thousand Raindrops	32
Finch	34
Gentians	35
No Imminent Danger	36

Luminosity

Every Fire Is Stolen	41
Still Life with Oranges	42
Das a Luz	44
Snow Work	45
Sound Barrier	46
Particle	47
The Painter of Niaux	48
February Day	50
Quilting with Buddha	51

Late Spring under Whitehouse Mountain	52
On Discovering a Single Sprout with Two Leaves	53
Shooting Stars at Ghost Ranch	54
Seventeen Ways of Saying Rain	55
Blue Norther	56
Solstice	57
Van Gogh at the Café Terrace in Arles, 1888	58

Certainty

Chance	63
Grass Song	64
Poppies	65
Insight into the Second Law of Thermodynamics	66
Animal Ways	67
The Bear Woman	68
Monsoon Season	69
I Reread an Old Poem	70
Dark Matter	71
Security Line	72
Summer 1968	74
Last Time	75
To Let the World Go	77
Entropy	79
Erasure	81
There Is No Silent Place	83

Notes
About the Author

Immensity

*Lost somewhere between immensity and eternity is
our tiny planetary home.*
—Carl Sagan

Remember to look up at the stars . . .
—Stephen Hawking

Driving the Pass

Two slim lanes and no guardrail, only
road to take me south from the Colorado
mountain town I call home. Inside

massive walls of ruby sandstone
hold back by net places rock falls;
outside steep bouldered banks drop

to a creek, rubble and snow-filled
into summer, not near enough
to cushion a rollover. Someone

dies here almost every year why others
drive the center line, white-knuckled,
counting hairpin curves, mile markers

to Ironton's wide valley where the way
widens to gravel shoulder and low grass.
Here I've learned to live with danger,

shift and slide, know avalanche is a season.
And chances I once took for love or wealth
I forget, all my older fears recede.

Today a cobalt sky stretched high and far
over red cliffs is a prayer to stay between
the yellow stripes and absent verge

on four small wheels, in glass and steel, for gravity
to hold me through the pass, all space unknown.
Just breathe in the thin air and don't look down.

Reflection on the Universal Law of Gravitation

Earth has its way to call us home
from mountain sides, heights,
thrones, stardom, or states of grace,
gravity that fixes a sure trajectory

for moons, stars and planets,
all bodies in the Universe,
even for astronauts probing space,
boulders, fly balls, ballerinas.

In a whirling world sometimes
you land hard, trip sidelong on a stair,
face-plant down an icy run;
it's not fate but law that bruises knees.

A player jumps, reaches out for the catch,
dancer turns high *tour jeté*—
neither can stop motion, suspend
the moment before the drop.

How this force of attraction
beneath field and hardwood floor
keeps us in our native place
like Newton who stood fixed,
lens at a window in 1680
yet travelled the firmament.

One time, too, sudden as an avalanche,
you and I fell in love,
slipped on a smile, a word, a touch
and descended onto a new terrain
with no map or compass,
promising to hold onto each other
in the unstoppable spinning.

Exoplanet

An artist shaped you much like Earth
                land sphere with blue water, larger girth
otherwise quite similar to it, circling
                round a dwarfish sun that could birth life
nearly 500 light years from us.
                Kepler 186f astronomers say
they saw your shadow darken stars
                you have a briefer year, a longer day
not too warm or too cold, sibling planet
                orbiting in a zone called *Goldilocks*
far off other world in our universe
                with water possible for plants and trees
with animal life, perhaps humanoid peers
                a rock like Earth with gravity
giving us comfort we are not alone
                your existence not unlike our own.

Ice Lakes

I dreamed I walked between two lakes
circled by mountains and endless sky.

Below me long and grassy steeps
fell into a basin of willow brakes.

When we reached the first blue lake
(or was it a fragment of summer sky?)

I held onto a narrow path,
my feet climbed over fallen scree

hands gripped outcrops of tumbled rock.
The higher second lake was green

with an knobby island of brown earth
out in the middle that some of us

swam to, the water brisk and deep.
On the way back down to trees and road

rocks, flowers, lakes stayed behind.
Only the wide sky followed me.

Immensity

Magnitude, enormous expanse
or volume; earth's oceans

in their deep profundity,
silent, rough, random, fixed

by laws of chaos and swirl;
vastness, boundless extent

as the immensity of endless
emptiness anchored

in space by shiny studs of stars,
distant others birthing, merging,

burning to black holes
throughout the darkness of space;

space-time's fabric supporting
my body, actions, thoughts,

tying the circling moon to Earth,
holding planets captives of Sun;

all that came before me/
and all that will come after me.

To William Blake one thought
could fill it.

Tree Line

We feel taller now, more vulnerable
two hours up when we stop for rest
after spruce forest, meadows, streams
we cross, trees grown scrawny
and fewer, earth gravelly,
gentian and moss campion
where mountain divides
between tree and not-tree.

Everything in the Universe
is breaking apart or coming together.
Add up all the pluses and minuses
and you still get vast green cirque,
mute rock, distant summit,
truths I consider, urging
one booted foot in front of the
other, breaths faster, frequent.

What we call blue seems so far,
so high, all space here and beyond
nothing but force fields
we are passing through,
naming places matter masses
apple, boulder, blossom, scree.

You tell me Einstein once said
people climb mountains
to get a better view
of what they do not know
or have not yet imagined. I answer
supernovae, black holes, forgiveness.

As trail turns to steep slope
we plod on past tree line,
our bodies' work the day's play
between matter and energy,
attention and earthly love,
praying the forces that push and pull
will also bring us back down.

Wolves

    after Ted Hughes

The wolves are howling tonight
        above U.S Highway 40,
Kremmling a world without
        coniferous woodland, deep
valley on the cusp of spring,
        edge of aspen grove, ice-crusted creek
they cross, southward wandering.

A video camera near Walden
        captured one, pale gray and tan,
black-tipped tail straight out,
        small pointed ears up, running
on long legs across an open field.
        Frozen mud tracks of *canis lupus*
attest it was young, no match for
        a .22 rifle, big rig, subdivision.

When wind sweeps down
        the hunched wolf shivers,
marking scent for the pack,
        scat on the shady forest floor.
Traveling at night it sees
        with golden eyes by snow and stars,
by day glints of a rancher's barbed wire.

Earth under its feet, tongue
        the wolf breeds, feed its young,
living only to gather, hunt prey
        to not starve in the darkness.
To not feel the steel trap
        like bared teeth, bones crack
in a final clashing.

It is the hour of the wolf
        and they are howling
that they live like this,
        drawing up and out
their long ropes of sound
        the owl hears with its delicate ear.

The wolves are howling tonight
        we cannot say whether
out of agony or joy.

All or Nothing

Nothing will do but to admit
there is a lot of you, nothing,

expanding, curving, exploding, birthing
throughout the Universe, without ceasing,

shape shifter with no mass or charge—
there is just no way to measure you.

Big zero. Nil. Nada.
Our best thinkers can't detect you

but only suspect you are behind
every insect wing, giant redwood,

fiery star and human being,
lurking between every atom,

holding together everything that exists.
Before Einstein you were named

Ether and *Vacuum*
but some now say you are eleven strings

of nothing (or maybe shards of subatomic particles).
I think I'll call you *invisible glue.*

Both absence and presence,
you are the hole inside the empty bucket,

biblical void, wholly ghost,
suffused with unknown potential,

proof something comes from nothing.
Without you everything would be lost.

You are the white paper for my uncertain pen.
You are the air I step through above this broken sidewalk.

Each Life Converges to Some Centre

The heavens turn out to be a photographic plate
of cosmic history, South Pole the darkroom
telescope's antenna our imagination

Universe a swath of sky and stars
14 billion light-years across
where remote radio signals reveal

themselves in the fabric of space-time
like light ruffling black taffeta
or air wrinkling the skin of a lake,

formed at the primordial moment
less chaotic Bang than explosive bubble.
Picture this: waves of gravity compete

for room, spin to the breaking point,
dark energy reverses and wrenches
quantum particles in a violent torque

to a runaway expansion, then balloons
out into space our own and all other galaxies.
Surer for the distance these faint patterns

sent from the newborn Universe
appear like a much-faded message
on the back wall of the cosmos

little spirals on a screen of microwaves,
ancient sliver of space-time saved for us
mysterious as the Shroud of Turin.

Eternity enables the endeavoring
to dare . . . to reach . . . we are beyond the stars
we mark tonight in space unknown so far.

At the Great Gallery

We catch breath when we finally see
        those armored giants, great panoply
to wonder at. Who painted them
        two thousand years ago or more
                and why high on an alcove's stone?

God, man or shaman wears the crown
        with armless body, shield-like shape
painted blood-red on lighter rock,
        mystery of designs incised,
                marching with others in a line.

We share the language water knows
        beneath these tall red sandstone walls
where we take in sage-scented air,
        shelter from the noonday sun
                in a grove of cottonwoods.

Remote museum or place of bones
        long gone to dust? What words were said
or sung, sacred or quotidian?
        Whose whispers on the wind?

Only the hidden canyon knows,
        its sheer swirled sides carved eons deep
where new footsteps mark streambed damp
        along curves of sand and shallow seep.

Solo Hiking, Utah

Silent spires fill sight
light rises on red bluffs

buttes and blue sky
climb to cairns cross

slick rock fins wind-faced
grasp bend and tread

grip and scale boulders
scrape body to rock face

then stem and press chest
against walls or walk

on knees, reel and breathe
deep air. In a layered

and pocked slot of knotted
tree roots lift hips from the slit

when boots slip then
slide down lichened stone

sides of time-molded folds
and crab-crawl across ledge

edges sensing each measure
of descent to sand dune

noon oasis of old juniper
shade to a curved cave

where wind whispers time
and an arch opens like an eye.

The Heart of Matter

Now we know everything we know
is stitched together of electrons and quarks,
tiny *ménages a trois* named

up, down, top, bottom, charm or *strange*
in a psychedelia of red, green, blue
particles behaving more like waves.

Quarks and gluons forming
protons and neutrons, leptons
becoming electrons and neutrinos

this whole choir of fermions
carried through the aisles of existence
by heaped legions of bosons

including a new one called *Higgs*
physicists finally caught up with.
So much exists we do not see:

the Universe in its blind vastness,
a magnitude of numbers
we struggle to comprehend

space-time's fourth dimension
that marks our human life span
Earth's gravity that comforts us

and a force magnetic that draws us
as it did young Einstein
when sick in bed he turned

in his hands a small compass.
Petal, feather, table, moth wing:
how can one field permeate

the whole of creation and hold us
small fish in our earthly tank?
What I know this summer night:

one tenuous moment of our being
subtle rhythms of our heartbeats
atoms of our cells merging with

quivering uncertainty, the quanta
inside us and everywhere elusive
and mysterious as faith or love.

Ten Thousand Raindrops

In Cheng-tu in poor health
        and thin patched robe, Tu-fu

sat by the window of his
        thatch roofed cottage,

ink and brush on the table,
        watching rain fill the mountain

streams, bamboo shoots and pine
        starts green hillsides

where egrets flapped like blowing
        snow across the peaks.

Plum rains he called them
        for the yellow fruit.

Rain leaked over the sill. Two orioles
        perched inside a branch.

What more could a simple man ask?
        Tu-fu wrote.

The children making fishhooks
        at his feet. His wife

brewing pungent teas
        of *ma huang* and *reishi*.

When wind drives spring rains
        into our valley, I look out at

bending iris, soaked horses in the fields,
    the running ditches, my face

in the wet glass streaming,
    my loved ones distant,

notebook and pen close by. *Spirit-wounded,*
    we both cannot stop our gazing.

Finch

Sometimes the wind blows terribly here.
New snow covers my shoulders, cheeks
redden in the cold, eyes tear but I do not
cry. Other times the air is still except for
the fluttering of small birds from bare
branches to drifted earth. At dawn and
noon I hear only silence when I hold out
my begging bowl and open my plain heart
to the lead-filled skies. But silvery trout
still swim under the frozen skin of the
river and here on the snow-laden porch
the rosy chest of a house finch glistens.

Gentians

Along a high meadow path
        above the firs and pines

past white rocks
        some big as miners' cabins

the mountain gentians
        unfurl five pointed petals

of such deep blue
        the ink maker only dreams.

Bend your face into their slim leaves
        amid the wild grasses and

you see some keep tight closed, waiting
        for mid-day sun.

If you return by the same lucky path
        the gentians open their blue bottles

as when the poet Li Po dipped his brush
        earth and sky joined.

No Imminent Danger

Sometimes things, people
disappear without a trace,

into a black hole we learned
to say from scientists

who say there are ten million
in the Milky Way galaxy

no imminent danger to us
like global warming,

guns in theaters.
Still black holes lurk

around dark corners
numerous as grains of sand,

a new one born every time
a large star runs out of fuel,

dies, cools to a dense core.
Hate living on after the anger fades.

No light can escape inside
them, the pull of gravity

so relentless the usual laws
break down. Super-massive

absences acting like presences.
My father dead these ten years

speaks to me still.
Good news for Earth, our

sun too small to be drawn into
a black hole. We humans

lucky enough specks
in the great inexhaustible

becoming. And some say
black holes can give birth

to whole new galaxies, loaded
with so much matter and energy.

Imagine all those exploding
stars and holes calling

to one another. Like us
with apologies, vows, fresh

starts, clamoring for another
chance to get things right.

Luminosity

For the rest of my life I will reflect on what light is.
—Albert Einstein

My body is light.
—Tu-fu

Every Fire Is Stolen

In the moments before dawn, light
        glows pewter, then
    lavender, then rose, light
travelling from the sun's fiery
        corona to beam across
    the bedcovers a narrow shaft
of brightness that left only minutes
        ago. The same light gleams
    gold the snow on Mount Abram's
peak, then steals across the room
        in visible shade patterns,
    unleashed waves of photons
I cannot see, light that broke
        for the first time when
    the Universe was only 300,000
years old. Billions of years later
        we still see by it, light that
    speeds immense distance, guides
and sparks streets, light that makes
        a pearl of the moon, kindles
    edges of waves on shore, shines
through new leaves, inside
        raindrops, illumines the face
    of a child, light that rests red
on the rim of the indigo sea before
        it slips from sight. Light, healer
    in our dark hours, you remind me
of what I do not see or cannot
        bear to see, you enter me
    even in my bandaged places.

Still Life with Oranges

In my language your color is your name,
color of hearth flame and hillside poppies.

Here you are *portokali*, sweet yield of Portugal.
In my palm you are a bright world

I curl fingers around, perfect globe.
I revolve you between your axes

of little stem and navel,
omphalos out of which Zeus birthed.

Or are you a full moon rising
after the *ergates* burn brush in the fields

smoking the spring air above the dusty groves
that line the narrow roads outside Mystras?

Neruda called you sun with fiery rind,
a single wheel of golden ingots,

borne from the Indian to the Mediterranean,
fruit that feeds sailors and all the senses.

I roll you in my hands, peel skin
until my fingers hold the taste of you.

Then from each spoke flows a clean bite
and your juice spills into my mouth

freedom songs of the Peloponnese.
One evening below Mt. Taygetus

how your brilliant hue lit the dark trees
inside their shiny-leaved branches

when I climbed a wooden ladder
to fill a cotton bag I wore against my chest.

Later I dreamed Ritsos stood
at the door with a full basket.

Morning's bowl of new-picked fruit
on a table covered by blue cloth,

you are *proino* for high-stepping soldiers.
Last night you were white blossoms

perfuming a courtyard with secrets
high above the unconquerable seas.

Das a Luz

You and I drove through the desert night
in a dark car—the pale dawn was our light.

We once walked down a mountain by light
the full moon made, sheltered by light.

Billions of years the Universe sends its light.
Tracking meteors at the shore I lay in light..

When Buddha breathed his last day in the light
he said to those with ears, *You are the light.*

Nights in his room the child asks for a light,
a door cracked, mother's voice the same as light.

What did my father say on his last night?
It was *Michael*, my brother, his life's light.

Das a luz— you give a baby to the light—
how much she tries to live into the light.

Snow Work

The man driving the snowplow
      whistles   happy inside
his glass and steel cubicle   as he heaps
      fresh snow onto the sloped
shoulder of County Road 17   and if
      more falls during the night
he will get out of bed   softly   won't
      awaken his wife   put on
a red-checked hat   old leather gloves
      climb into the truck
retrace unseen tracks beneath
      yellow headlights.

An artist with snow his drifting impasto.

In the shadow of a French winter
      Pissarro painted on white-primed
canvas   barren trees   blue ice
      slate sky   the lonely road
from Versailles to Louveciennes
      in *plein aire*   heavy wool coat
replenishing   laying open again
      the thick landscape.

How   in the cold dawn   they ply on
      through bleakness
only sound   the plow's hum and stroke
      lifting into snow-laden pines.

Sound Barrier

In the middle of the day
there was a loud crack
and boom and we saw
a white streak in the blue
sky outside the kitchen
window where Mother
stood at the sink as a
blast shook our whole
house, rattled dishes in
the cupboards, shattered
a water glass on the wet
edge of the sink while we
stared speechless, Mother
and I, who knew little of
light speed and sound
waves in the summer of
1953 when they broke it.

Particle

A small bit, so small
as to barely be seen;
part of something larger;
part of a whole;
from the Latin *particular*;
A particle of dust
in a shaft of sunlight.

A minute portion of matter;
an object with mass
but without size;
subatomic particle,
proton, neutron, or electron;
elementary particle;
lepton, muon, Higgs boson.

A particle acts like a wave,
a wave like a particle.
I am made of particles
of water and salt;
my body moves in waves.

An object existing in a dualism
between the continuous
and the discontinuous.

A particle has being and motion;
a particle is real;
it is a theory.
It is all things;
it is no one thing.

A particle is only part of the truth.

The Painter of Niaux

He saw by torch inside this craggy
Ariège hilltop, one hand lighting
his way over wet cave floor.

The other gripping limestone walls,
basket of tools. This narrow passageway,
dampness, uneven steps we follow,

eyes growing used to shade, to depth.
A shadow in his Romanesque apse,
lone artist save for spirits, gods?

Water beneath us, we breathe earth,
see only what he knew, cambered
walls, ibex he hunted, bison,

in whispers marvel at curves in stone,
shoulders, rumps, upturn of horns,
Chagall's cow, a bull, Picasso's.

Master of two horses running,
he laid one atop the other
legs outstretched, their hoofed feet,

this image from a wintering valley.
Did his lamp waver beside the wall
while he shaped lines to numinous?

And you, what would you have done
for hunger's cries, the arrow's success?
The painter did not leave a name

but time left us these silent strokes
we trace in air, a shining mane
limned on undulating rock.

February Day

Snow fattens porch chairs and tables,
>everything rounded off
into what wind and crystal
>overnight have molded.

Frozen water particles reflecting light
>from inside airy molecules
fall soundless, become cover
>cornice, dune, drift.

How the whitened air hides mountain
>and wood and river;
how the winter garden meditates
>over its blurred heaps.

In this much snow you lose bearings
>look for sight lines in fence posts,
a ghost row of ditch cottonwoods,
>listen for the *om* of a snowplow.

Quilting with Buddha

What a fine steel needle
with an eye like a cricket's
and strong cotton thread
you give me to sew this cloth
into a useful blanket
of colors and patterns
various as a field
of summer wildflowers.

Up and down, in and out
the needle moves my fingers
as winds hem the clouds,
first swallows stitch the sky
The world is never at rest
so you must quiet the mind.

If you work with me
while the good light lasts,
I'll brew green tea for us
and we'll drink together
from these blue china cups.

Late Spring under Whitehouse Mountain

Pine trees grow
like great candles
on the steep hillside
as if placed there by the faithful,
light now circling around us
longer and wider each day,
summoning all that's alive
up from moist earth,
roots spreading under fields,
forest floor and banks
of the plummeting river.

Li Po said his heart grew
rich with repose
when he wandered
under the mountain,
no noise, no confusion
in the empty trees,
and in spring
even the robe he wore
was woven of emeralds.

On Discovering a Single Sprout with Two Leaves

Fill birdbath with water for bluebirds
        set out deck chairs
hang winter duvet over a railing
        then feel sun through shirtsleeves
smell warming-up earth
        count cars heading for the open pass
listen for the river running full with snowmelt.

Keep watch each day for a falls
        to plunge from a cleft in the red cliffs
its white plume you'll take for a sign
        though trees are still bare and wild
grasses lying brown and prostrate.

How you lived inside yourself
        through cold nights of longing
hearing only wind creak, hearts break, dreaming
        like Rengetsu, who shattered ice
to draw water, imagining a field of violets.

Now you want to bare your whole body
        burn in the grate what's left of sorrow
offer in your hands what remains—
        fragrant leaf mold, adobe mud
budding tips of old branches.
        You walk everywhere on tiptoes.

Shooting Stars at Ghost Ranch

What is it we are a part of we do not see?
—Loren Eiseley

Such brightness in the immense
blackness I try to comprehend.
A Universe 13 billion years old,
space-time, curved with strings
that sound in ten dimensions,
transparent matter holding together
billions of stars and planets.

          This August night
I only know Earth I call *home*
is orbiting through a far-off field,
bits and pieces of comet rock
slamming into our atmosphere
lighting up nighttime.
Brilliant Perseid meteors
more than fifty we count
an hour, their persistent trains
lacing across the constellations
in a New Mexican sky on top of
a sleeping mesa where we sit
in a small galaxy of armchairs
and I murmur to you *Ohhh*
as each passes over our heads,
falling, burning itself up and out.

Seventeen Ways of Saying Rain

      Rain that makes the yellow leaves fall, rain that drips from a downspout into the mint patch, rain that beats a tattoo on the metal roof, rain that soaks through a waterproof jacket, rain that hangs like small pearls on spruce branches, rain that turns river water to café au lait, rain that collects on the backs of black and white cows, rain on marsh marigolds that was snow yesterday, rain that rolls rocks down onto a mountain pass, rain that makes dust puffs rise from dry earth, rain that shines through July afternoon sunlight, rain that smells of wood stacks and wood smoke, rain that hisses on asphalt under truck wheels, rain that unearths mushrooms in the forest, rain that paints deep red the sandstone cliffs, rain that bends down the faces of sunflowers, rain that mingles with tears.

Blue Norther

Means cold wind that sweeps
from the western plains south,
sure sign of winter.

It swirls leaves and duff
from black oaks and cedar elms
on stick-littered paths cut

through dun dry grass, turns mud
frost-hard. Bends bushes by
a rippling creek where purple

callicarpa berries cling.
Mountain-bred, I feel myself
a stranger here, over-exposed

under skies that hang heavy,
gray as old sheets until cold sun leaves
them rose-tinted at the front door.

When night steals in the blue
chill deepens over the blown fields.
Like *animas perdidos* bare boughs

beat against rain-wet windows
while inside we kindle a first fire
and practice *hold fast.*

Solstice

Ice grips road edges
steel-silvery and slick
where snowmelt frozen

tree branches whistle brittle
in frigid wind, crowns bare
as hoary heads, old ashes

wait cold in the grate
dusk's pause before dark
enters the unlit window

bids me *be still*
then settles in silence
over house and field.

This night let us hold
onto stars' broken beacons
the ruins of moonlight

until shadows draw back
and, to our beckoning, sun's
bright flame again bends.

Van Gogh at the Café Terrace in Arles, 1888

My dear Theo,
In this small room as I smoke my pipe
accordion music from *Place Lamartine*

fills my ears. I think of my lost love Caroline
and also of Clasine, my own sweet Sien.
When at *onze heures* the *Place du Forum*

begins to empty of late revelers,
I carry down into the street
my heavy easel and paint box.

I tell you I am better each blue day
I go out into the fields of poppies
where sometimes children follow me

and my burdens grow less.
You would like this hour at the café
when only a few patrons sit over their wine

while *le garcon* slowly wipes clean
the porcelain tops of the iron tables.
L'aire du Sud grows cooler

and wind gentles the chestnut leaves
that cast shadows over the stones.
As always I remain grateful for the paints

you send me from Tanguys. This yellow
I used for my sunflowers makes light
pour out on the dim *terrasse*

as from a lantern just inside the door.
See how it turns the cobbles pink and leaves
the gables of houses in violet darkness?

I especially thank you for the deep blue
I will use to paint the sky before I hang
on it a few of the uncountable stars.

I hope you are well and also your dear Jo
and little Vincent as well as our *Maman*.
Mon Dieu, I am fatigued. My hands

stiffen at this late hour, yet I feel such lucidity!
All doubting voices float into the immensity
and here is hope or God.

Certainty

Every country is death's.
       —Jane Hirshfield

Why love what you will lose? There is nothing else to love.
       —Louise Gluck.

Chance

That my sister was born
with a murmuring heart
but I was not. That
it whispered deep inside her
sshh, sshh, sshh with every beat
until one night a valve stopped,
small dam that finally failed.

That a surgeon cracked her breast open
like an egg, her heart the vital yolk
he probed and patched for hours,
its finger-sized hole. That later
we both cried when she showed me
the line of ragged, bluish stitches.

That love comes to any of us
even when we are unmindful.
That the miracle is we breathe in,
breathe out, arms and bodies
opening, closing around each other,
answering *yes* and *yes*.

Grass Song

All the wild grasses are singing today—
their sound low, undulating,

their words a mantra for endurance.
Through long stems, a shallow sea,

I walk where wind bends their light—
here are big bluestems, sturdy seed heads

like turkey feet, thick spikes of wheatgrass
green needle grass, yellow Indian

and along the road, silvery brome.
From small seeds borne by birds, animals

or carried by wind for centuries, their rhizomes
spread slow beneath valley and foothill.

Rooted even in rocky soil they hold onto,
grasses thrive in wet years, survive in the dry.

I wonder if my roots are here as well
being a wanderer so long

before I called mountains home.
Some years they don't grow this high

and in drought years stalks turn brown,
die before first frost or snow

lays them low. Yet even in winter, stiffened
and white, all the wild grasses whisper, *Stay.*

Poppies

How this sea of disordered blooms
scents the wind, silk on my fingers

fragile petals that fall into my palm
revealing their black, secret hearts.

Field of red poppies that opens
between green hill and hedgerow,

from distance a child's crayon strokes,
lipstick smears over the spring grass

of the Aragon, up close each one
a pointillist's little flame.

Lorca, before he was struck down,
wrote of *la violete matiz* of poppies,

color of the blood of young men
and women killed in *La Guerra*.

Las amapolas grow still in broken places—
sprout from earthen cracks in the white

limestone walls of the abandoned church
where we stop, eat bread, pungent *olivos*.

Each scarlet cluster whispers *Remember this*
springing from rocks along the path we climb

where groves of almond trees are soldiers
at rest in the snow of their flowers.

Insight into the Second Law of Thermodynamics

Watch cumulus clouds strew
        billows in a blue July sky
and hear raindrops beat on the roof
        a tangled afternoon tattoo.

See how fallen rocks litter a mountain
        where wildflowers grow haphazard
and winds tousle varicolored leaves
        to a medley at the fence.

How sea waves' tumult forms
        random gestures in wet sand
where tumbled pebbles and shells
        scatter on the land.

How snow crystals, not ever alike,
        dance in spots of winter light
and the splintered stars, the ones we see,
        glitter all night indiscriminately.

Animal Ways

The cries of coyotes in the night
woke me up halfway between
hope and dread, that shadowed place.

Or was it the hungry mountain lion
screaming at a yearling kill?
Outside the bright and silent moon

hooked a curtain of black sky,
deep snow reflected borrowed light
on field and fence, and empty branches

of the barren oaks gave way to wind.
I walked uneasy through the silent house
and sleep did not come for me again.

By morning's calm snow had filled
the footprints of the animals,
on one small drift a scarlet smear

almost concealing that wild cache,
and into the slow-moving river
white-covered hills had fallen.

The Bear Woman

That was the end of nights they roamed
down from the woods, the night we heard
echo down valley the rifle shots.

Snow just gone, roots, forbs and cones
were plenty to paw and tongue and chew
and a summer moon in the clearing shone.
Their dark hair matted with needles and duff,
not sated, slow-footed, they made their way
to kibble or scraps the woman put out.

The bears grew used to the rise and fall
of her voice, a back door opening,
her steps on the wooden porch,
smells of grease in the clothes she wore.

She lived all year to hear and watch
their clowning growls and shoves up close
and sometimes reached to touch one's head,
thick-muscled back, the forest on him,
and felt no fear of his mouth-warmed breath.

Death would always wait, she thought.
Then a slash, the grass, and the world went red,
woman and bears finally caught
outside a cage of pine, unlatched.

Monsoon Season

Sometimes in summer rain drops briefly
        against the nearby aspen trees
and sunshine climbs the ropes of it.

Sometimes thunder groans in the distance
        or rumbles louder, deeper
when too-close lightning shakes the house.

Sometimes a storm passes quietly
        into another valley, hanging against
the cliffs a silent scrim of cloud.

Sometimes rain settles, stays into evening,
        pounds steady on roof and field,
whipping branches against the windows.

Sometimes I let go of all other expectations
        and desires and sit under the porch eaves
breathing the scent of sodden grass

where I watch purple coneflowers bend
        in the garden, where in a wooden barrel
I've learned to catch whatever falls.

I Reread an Old Poem

Words spring out
of their assigned places:

mountain moves away from *hawk*
next replaces *last*
enough flies to the margin near *trouble*.

Zealous letters fidget and fight
for more white space—

*C i r r u s   t h r e a d e d
sk i e s   o p e n .*

All syntax betrays—
periods fly off into high peak limbo

commas come unhooked
like fingerling trout

former thoughts no longer hold the ground.

Dark Matter

Everything exists that ever was,
        all matter we see in the Universe
                that sprouts, wanders, shines

but so much more than what
        we know of the cosmos
                dark matter we now suspect

source of intense gravity
        is keeping stars, planets, us
                from flying out into space

tugging on our own and every
        galaxy like a dog on a leash,
                holding the whole glittering in

balance, mysterious, ubiquitous
        web of unknown particles
                scientists struggle to define

that neither lets light in nor out,
        matter dark and elusive as
                a symptom without a diagnosis,

my unspoken thoughts, hidden sins
        all things I think I know
                governed by what I do not.

Security Line

Sometimes you're asked to prove
who you are. So you open your wallet,

take out a card with your photo
that lists your name and residence,

height, weight, blue eyes, brown hair.
So much more is not there:

the burdens your hands have held,
from your lips, what words, scars

below your navel and one nipple.
When the officer looks in your eyes

above her black-framed glasses,
you answer *Yes, yes*, as with her gloved hand

she motions you through the gate.
There are some others with your name

(you recently checked on Facebook)
a realtor, lawyer, pediatrician

but they're not on the Burbank flight.
When you got your first passport,

marriage license, job at the college
you had to show a printed paper

you keep folded in an envelope
that has on it an inked footprint

smudgy, the size of half your thumb
(this evidence, too, is surely you)

a certificate embossed in gold that stated
your name, officially signed and dated

in the courthouse of a Midwest town
where you will never return.

Summer 1968

    after Charles Simic

You were young and green
when you first learned about the Buddha
when you wore your brown hair long and turned on
to the Revolution, street life and the
music of sitars. You knew this was the fruit,
the karma of your life before. You could stand
in your sandals on a corner all day. Your sign said we
love you and you handed out flowers and could eat
a meal on what people gave you. The
others said it was because of your smile.
You called them your sisters and
brothers you lived with on a little spit
of land with cypress trees and sand that stuck out
into the Pacific just above Santa Cruz. The
boy you slept with had such white teeth.

Last Time

My father has his arm around Jane,
his second wife,
on the gray front porch.
They are smiling, dressed
for summer in white short sleeves.
I am the oldest daughter
who is holding the camera
in front of their beach house,
my young son beside me
not in the picture.

All afternoon we sit in chairs
under a maple tree's shade.
They smoke their cigarettes
and I try to keep the talk going
of this summer's drought,
a niece's marriage, their new internist,
Andrew in my sight down
where the blue sound meets sand.

At night over plates of shrimp,
my father at the table's head
smiles often, nursing his one drink,
telling jokes and old stories.
His hair's gone all white,
his face still smooth and ruddy.
I think it is so much easier
for him to love my son.

Later when we go to bed
Dad leaves an upstairs window open
and a small light turned on
so if we wake up in the night
we'll remember we're at his house
on the Connecticut shore.

To Let the World Go

She's shrunk like an oft-washed doll, body frail.
When she leans on me, I fear she'll fall
she weighs so little, her petite dress

from Vermont Country touches the floor.
She looks up, whispers, *You've cut it short for summer,*
blue eyes like mine don't miss my hair.

I miss the voice that once sang mezzo solos,
oratorios, kept me to assignments, kitchen chores,
take one trembling hand, beringed, arthritic

don't hug hard so not to bruise thin skin.
Mother tells me she is happy in one room
with a high bed that leans back like a chaise,

Bible, prayer book, phone on a side chest.
Says, *They let my have my breakfast in my room.*
Someone helps her bathe, brushes her hair

my sisters and I never could do very well.
When I push her wheelchair to the library,
the dining room, foyer with Starbucks coffee,

she tells me fans watch Giants games together,
Says, *Did you know I take a painting class on Fridays?*
In Friends House at 92 she's making new ones

so many of those she had already dead.
Ten years ago Mother gave my son her Honda,
long before gave me her Winter piano,

later she stopped shopping, emailing me.
I asked for her gold bracelet, antique book ends,
a neighbor got her desk of fifty years,

pots, linens, all her books went to Goodwill.
Mother is letting go things of this life.
Has she begun to let the world go, even me?

This sadness I can't speak of in the courtyard,
Mother sitting in the sun at Scrabble,
right hand shaking an *O,* switches to left.

Entropy

Here winds shift in random paths,
mountains crumble to gravel,

water falls over the lip of a cliff,
still green stream dropping to frenzy.

All is energy stored up breaking free—
ice puddles, skillet fat scalds,

cream swirls in my coffee mug,
a wineglass shatters to shards

atoms that will not rebond.
How life keeps every particle

in motion, disperses all energy
the Universe birthed—

even at rest my body seeks
energy, sucks oxygen

and will until my last breath,
death the extreme of entropy.

Some liken it to disorder, chaos,
that unpredictable sister's

room cluttered with clothing,
messy desk of a former boss.

Nerve impulses switching routes,
cells mutating to deadly blooms,

seagull's wing stirring the storm.
A log burns red in the grate,

pine becoming ember, smoke, ash
that for decades shed cones and needles

through sun, rain, snow—this slow decay
I sense in wrinkled face, hands, the mind's delay.

Time's arrow steals all things we know and love,
every complex system fickle, fractal, bending.

It takes the path of least resistance, inevitable
as life's fragile journey, steely as law.

Erasure

You walk uphill in silent snow
between silhouettes of pines

where everything is ice-clear—
the creek, rimed rocks, frozen

branches of willows. So much
we think we know can be lost—

yesterday, this moment, 15 billion
brain cells 100 billion stars

in the galaxy. Somewhere we store
the scent of wet wool, soup on gray

days, cracks in sidewalks, an old
wallpaper pattern. A child's

mementos carried in her pocket
later require luggage, boxes of books,

a rental trailer pulled into a new town,
van across the desert to California

where a rented bungalow holds
everything until it takes two stories,

eight rooms, so much space for
a future. How the years fill with

the work of living, energy and matter
switching places partway between

love and death. Now *downsize* is
the new word to keep what matters

most, you study Zillow for two
bedrooms, walk-in closet, close

market, read synapse retrieval slows,
a brain runs out of niches. This morning

you can't recall where the snow-covered
path forks, why five planets align,

the name of a distant peak against
the blue. Two deer browsing lift heads,

your eyes meet briefly before the forest
takes them back as if they never were.

There Is No Silent Place

Though I listened in a forest glade.
It was hushed save for wind shifts,
my footfalls on a needled path,
jay twitter from a pine, rustling dry leaves.
I could still hear my heart beating
inside its fleshly house, blood filling,
refilling little rooms built of 212 bones.

My mother listened more and spoke less
the days before she died. I held her hand
and knew she could not take me with her
into that long trough of darkness,
space-time of a different dimension.

I used to fear silence, being alone
in this place where cosmic noise of radio waves
makes music though our ears cannot hear
pitches and tones travel through the solar system.
Shock waves of the sun shrieking when
they collide with interstellar plasma.
Think nails on a chalkboard, rusted gates.

In a place we thought serene, comets fall
through magnetic fields, bits slipping off,
clicking like castanets, whistles eardrum-
breaking from Jupiter's lightning storms,
Saturn's poles singing like the sea.

Here on Earth soft soughs of spring winds
round corners of cottonwood trees,
trucks moan and thrum on the highway,
the river murmurs from across the road.

I can still hear her say my name.

Notes

"Wolves"
    Endangered and rare in Colorado, in April 2015 a gray wolf was shot and killed by a coyote hunter near Kremmling.

"Each Life Converges to Some Centre"
    Title and lines are taken from Emily Dickinson.

"Ten Thousand Raindrops"
    Tu-fu, celebrated poet of the Tang Dynasty, lived from 712 to 770.

"Every Fire Is Stolen"
    Title is taken from a poem by Jane Hirshfield.

"Still Life With Oranges"
    Yannis Ritsos (1909-1990) was a Greek poet, political activist, and World War II resistance fighter.

"The Painter of Niaux"
    The Grotte de Niaux in the foothills of the French Pyrenees is the site of prehistoric rock art determined to have been painted 14,000 years ago.

"On Discovering a Single Sprout with Two Leaves"
    Rengetsu was a Buddhist nun born in Kyoto in 1791.

"Seventeen Ways of Saying Rain"
    In the Japanese language there are seventeen words for rain.

"There Is No Silent Place"
    NASA Voyager spacecraft captured sounds of interstellar space from October to November 2012 and April to May 2013.

About the Author

Beth Paulson has been widely published over the last fifteen years in well over a hundred national literary journals and anthologies. Her poems have been three times nominated for Pushcart Prizes as well as Best of the Net. She has also been awarded prizes from West Side Books, Mesa State Festival, Mark Fischer Poetry Prize, *Cloudbank, The Eleventh Muse, Passager*, and the *Naugatuck River Review*. Her poetry has appeared in *Crazy Woman Creek: Women Rewrite the American West* (Houghton Mifflin, 2004), *What Wildness is This*: *Women Write About the Southwest* (University of Texas Press, 2007), *What's Nature Got To Do With Me?* (Native West Press, 2011), and *Going Down Grand: Poems from the Canyon* (Lithic Press, 2015). Beth's four previous collections are *The Truth About Thunder* (Ponderosa Press, 2001), *The Company of Trees* (Ponderosa Press, 2004), *Wild Raspberries* (Plain View Press, 2009), and *Canyon Notes* (Mount Sneffels Press, 2012). Beth taught English at California State University Los Angeles for over 20 years. She currently lives in Ouray County, Colorado where she leads Poetica, a workshop for area writers, and co-directs the Open Bard Poetry Series.